Texts
to the Holy

Also by Rachel Barenblat

70 faces: Torah poems
Waiting to Unfold
Toward Sinai: Omer poems
Open My Lips

the skies here
What Stays
chaplainbook
Through
See Me: Elul poems

Texts
to the Holy

Rachel Barenblat

Ben Yehuda Press
Teaneck, New Jersey

Published by Ben Yehuda Press
122 Ayers Court #1B
Teaneck, NJ 07666
http://www.BenYehudaPress.com

ISBN13 978-1-934730-67-6

21 20 19 18 / 10 9 8 7 6 5 4 3 2 1   20180204

≈

This book made possible
through the generosity of
Peggy Lin Duthie

in honor of
Rabbin Tom Cohen
and the congregation of
Kehilat Gesher, Paris

≈

Acknowledgements

Many of these poems originally appeared, sometimes in different forms or with different titles, on the blog Velveteen Rabbi. "Airport Havdalah" appeared in The Hineini Project's Sukkot booklet, fall 2015. "What Lasts" appeared in *Presence*, the journal of Spiritual Directors International, in June 2016. "Pray" appeared in *The Jewish Women's Literary Annual*, 2016. "Devotion" appeared in *What Canst Thou Say*, May 2016.

לשם יחוד קודשא בריך הוא ושכינתיה

for the sake of bringing-together
transcendence & immanence,
God far above & God deep within

and for the one who sees me

Contents

Your voice knocks

When I wake
your name is honey
on my lips.

All day long
you're with me.
My heart rests

in your hand.
I am safe
in your embrace.

You know
my innermost parts.
Nothing I say

nothing I am
could drive you
away from me.

Your voice knocks.
Like a magnolia
I open.

Longing, exit 16

Turn here
if your heart aches

if someone you love
is out of reach

if a beloved
is suffering

and you wish
more than anything—

Turn here
if you've wanted

what you didn't have
or couldn't have

if love overflows
like an open faucet

if yearning is as close
as you get to whole.

Rachel Barenblat

Light

Orange daylilies stand,
their crowd of upturned faces
gazing at the sun.

My heart knows that yearning.
Every cell in my body
calls out for you.

Night falls: my petals close.
I hug myself, bereft.
I count the hours until dawn.

I am most beautiful
when your radiance
draws forth mine.

My Torah

You're a tall drink of water
from the living well

the longer I know you
the more beautiful you become

I want to hold you close
and press my lips to your shoulder

to unfasten your gartel
with unsteady hands

to trace every letter
I find on your skin

you are milk and honey
on my tongue

anointing oil
on my hands

voice like flowing water
inscribing my heart

Rachel Barenblat

Texts to the holy

Shechina is riding shotgun.
Her toenails are purple.

She's tapping at her smartphone
sending texts to the Holy One.

What's it like, I ask her,
being apart? Do you wake up

melancholy and grateful
all at once, and fall asleep

thinking Shabbes can't come
soon enough, is always too short

you're always saying goodbye
and your own heart aches

to know he's hurting too?
And she looks at me

eyes kind as my grandmother
and timeless as the seas

and says, you tell Me, honey.
You tell Me.

Airport havdalah

Sun slides behind the concourse.
It's still today, but the coming week
encroaches. My mind clicks through
obligations like prayer beads.

Then the chat window opens.
The first words of havdalah:
Behold! The God of my redemption.
I open to the week; I am not afraid...

Suddenly though among strangers
I am not alone. You are with me.
Your emoji and your texts
—they comfort me.

As I board the plane
I catch a whiff of someone's perfume.
The seatbelt sign glows. In its light
my polished fingernails gleam.

Bless the One Who separates
and bridges. Even at a distance
we aren't really apart.
My cup overflows.

Rachel Barenblat

Morning blessing

When I have the luxury
of unhurried minutes with you

hands wrapped around
my morning mug of coffee

(flowing with milk and honey
because you are with me)

the sky becomes clearer, my heart
lighter, the road before me

streaked with joy
sings me a new song.

I seek your face

Show me your face
in the face in front of me.

Show me your light
in familiar eyes.

Show me your heart
in the overflowing of mine.

Show me how to be hollow
so you can pour through me.

Show me your name
written in the wheeling stars.

Show me my name
written across lifetimes.

In the face of my beloved
show me your face.

Rachel Barenblat

Gaze

I want to gaze at you
    not through lowered lashes
        protecting my tender places, but

heart splayed wide
    to everything I learn
        when I let myself be seen.

I want to gaze at you
    without flinching, knowing
        what you'll find in my eyes:

my aches and imperfections,
    the cracks in my clay heart,
        the tarnish clouding my silver.

I want to see all of you
    even if your pure light
        would burn out my circuits,

even if all I can glimpse
    is your shadowed silhouette
        through my sheerest tallit.

If I bring my whole self
    to yearning for you, if I seek
        to see and to be seen wholly

can I call forth
    the you who would be
        in relationship with me?

Rachel Barenblat

Promises

When it comes to you, dearest one,
I am profligate with promises:

I will remember you everywhere
I will open my eyes to you always

the channel between your heart and mine
will always be open, even when I ache

because you are too far away
or because my words fail me.

I wish I could adorn you with stars
but all I have are sparks

glinting between my cupped hands
cast by the tireless fire of my heart.

Secondhand

The exterior's a little shabby,
could use a coat of paint.

A bit worn after a hard year:
not a lot of curb appeal.

Most people walk right by.
Not you: you see

the mezuzah in the doorway,
the light in the living room.

You see my heart, tender
and afraid no one will ever want—

Tell me again that I'm worthy
even when I feel most broken.

Tell me again that my strength
is beautiful, and makes me whole.

Know

You know everything
there is to know.

Who I am; who I was
last time round.

How I carry myself
(eyes forward, head high)

when there's a chasm
gaping in my chest

and how my voice wavers
when I'm overcome with joy.

You know what I yearn for
even the parts I don't admit.

You know how much
beyond words means.

What you see

You make me want
to be better.

In your eyes
I become more.

No one else sees me
the way you do.

I see myself
through your eyes

and think: that's not
the me I know me to be.

It's the me I become
when I'm with you.

I want to be
what you see in me.

I can't hate you, but

sometimes I wish I could.
Fall asleep night after night
with your name on my lips

and wake the same way
and for what?
Offer you all that I have,

all that I am: offer you
my dedication and my heart
and you say nothing.

And when I draw up
all the courage I can find
and ask for what I need

you shrug and spread your hands.
Shame floods me with heat.
Stupid, to think I could have

what I yearn for. To forget
that you can't want me
the way I want you.

If I forget

How did I convince myself
that distance from you

didn't hurt?
That I didn't need

your song in my ear, melody
expanding my heart?

Worse: I told myself lies.
That my absence didn't pain you,

that I had nothing to give.
If I forget you, beloved—

let my fingers lose their grasp,
my throat unlearn how to sing.

Disconnecting from you
would mean shutting off

one of my senses, voluntarily
giving up breathing,

relinquishing a vitamin I need
in order to thrive.

Rachel Barenblat

After Sinai

For three glorious days
I'm with you on the mountain.
Face to face with your radiance
I remember how to shine.

I am seen. I open in places
I didn't know had been closed.
And then it's over. Even
in a crowd I feel alone.

I miss your voice so much
my own throat closes.
What I wouldn't give to be
in your sweet presence again.

Just this

Just this:
that you hear me.

You hear what I say
and what I leave unsaid.

You hear the stirrings
of my most hidden heart.

Just this:
no matter what I say

I'll never be
too much for you.

Because you hear me
I'm never alone.

Count

Times when
my wrenching fear
of disappointing you

made me close off
our connection—
I remember every one.

Times when
you've been as close to me
as my own heart,

when I've been
suffused with gratitude
all day long

because of
the mere fact of you—
too many to count.

Devotion

The devoted ones of old
    would spend a whole hour
        preparing to meet the Beloved

(a timeless time in union
    rocking back and forth
        murmuring words of love)

then an hour savoring
    the encounter now over,
        slowly letting afterglow fade.

As I get ready to greet you
    my soul, like theirs, sings
        in anticipation of being seen.

Our time together
    is always too short, though
        once gone I prolong it in memory.

I carry you with me.
    You fill the holy of holies
        in my innermost heart.

Rachel Barenblat

Not invisible

Being seen wholly
is more intimate
than any embrace.

Being known
beyond any pretense,
any veil I wear.

Gift beyond measure:
I don't have to hide
from your loving eyes.

You've forgiven me

I convinced myself
I didn't need you.

I made myself forget
how much sweeter

everything is
with you in it.

I was afraid
I wasn't enough.

And when I woke up
to how I need you

how I'm a better me
when I'm with you

there was no room
for shame between us.

Always already
you've forgiven me.

Rachel Barenblat

Remember

When I close my eyes
and when I open them again,

When I'm sitting at home
and when I'm out and about.

(I know I'm not supposed
to text and drive

but I send you notes anyway.)
Your name is written on my heart.

At every threshold
I remember you.

Learn

What I'm here to learn:
that it's okay
to take up space
with my ungainly heart.

That I deserve
a place at the table
and my mistakes
won't exile me.

That when you promised
love that transcends
all space and time,
you meant it.

Nothing to fear

You remind me
not to fear change.

Change is like breathing:
without it, death.

(Don't know where I'm going
but I can't stay here.)

You remind me
what stays the same:

my tender heart,
my love for you.

Pray

Sometimes I manage
formal conversation,
a love letter evening
and morning and afternoon

but most of the time
I rely on the chat window
open between us all day.
I want to tell you everything.

This month you are near.
Walk with me in the fields.
I want to take your hand
and not let go.

Rachel Barenblat

Toward you

Will it ever get easier?
Some days a black hole
takes up residence

in my ribcage
and swallows me
until all that's left

is yearning for you.
The ache threatens
to wash me away

but I can't hate it
because it points
toward you.

My heart, incomplete—
a piece of me is tucked
into your pocket.

Your heart, incomplete—
mine is enlivened
by a piece of you.

Your honor

With my heart in my hands
I approach the bench.

No: my heart
is in your hands.

You read me
like a book:

what I've said
and left unsaid

where I stumbled
over my own tangles

and where I shone
like the light of creation.

Only one thing do I ask,
this alone do I seek:

let me dwell
in your house, in your heart.

Please don't ever
hide your face from me.

Rachel Barenblat

Wake to you

I want to wake to you. When my alarm pulls me
(a silvered trout, struggling, from sleep's stream)

you remind me I breathe air, can thrive. Your song
calls forth my own. I'm a tuning fork, vibrating.

When my walls crumble and fall, you show me what stays.
Point out that shrinking myself won't keep me safe.

You take delight in my strength, urge me: be more.
You don't want artifice. You exult when I shine.

When I relinquish control at the end of day
and slip into sleep you keep me safe and seen.

In dreams I give you the keys to my secret places
but you don't need them: my door is open to you.

You know my true name. You know my tender heart,
the path into my garden where roses bloom.

The one who sees me

You are the one who sees me.
Please see me in soft focus.

This mirror shows only
what's worthy of scorn:

every flaw magnified
and stripped of holiness.

As imperfect as I am, how
can I find favor in your eyes?

Yet you watch over my planes
as they take off and land.

When I wake from bad dreams
you gentle my pounding heart.

Your voice quickens my pulse
and mends my broken places.

Your steadfast kindness
dissolves me like salt in water.

Help me believe you see me
more gently than I see myself.

Rachel Barenblat

Lamp

When grief has
   splashed my fire out,
      when my sanctuary

is dark, smeared
   with boot prints
      and wet ashes

when the holy of holies
   inside my rib cage
      is an aching void

It is you who wipe
   tears from my face
      with tender hands

who remind me
   I deserve better
      than desolation

who light my lamp.
   Bring me your flame.
      I want to shine again.

May it be

That after brokenness
comes repair.

That you'll always be
close as my heartbeat.

That we who sow in tears
will reap in joy.

That I never stop
knowing your beauty.

That I will live up
to your faith in me.

Rachel Barenblat

Intend

Only to stretch out
toward the sun; to bloom.

To unfurl my tender heart
like a banner billowing.

To draw water in joy
from the living well.

To open a channel
and let myself through.

Light

The moon wanes
and I ache.
Kindle a flame
against the dark.

If I can
say your name
even to myself
I'm not alone.

You remind me
that dwindlng hope
is the seed
of hope reborn.

Even down here
where I've fallen—
look: your light
is with me.

Can I awaken
you from below,
give you even
a measure of

what I receive?
Refracted between us—
what a blaze
might we shine?

Praise

For the meadow, softened
by the scrim of fog
and for sun burning through.

For the call
of black-capped chickadees
and for your voice

sealed
one lifetime to the next
in the soft wax of my heart.

For your name
written in me, gleaming
when I lift my hands to the light.

For the wonder
of not being alone,
the miracle of being enough.

Morning and evening

I wake (to awareness of you)
and am not alone: I bless.

Bless the early light
gilding the birch leaves, bless

the peach I cup in my hand
as tenderly as I would touch

your face. I seek your face.
Bless even the yearning, even

the ache. Bless the evening sky
blue as the one thread which winds

around the white, the thread
which binds me to you. Every knot

a blessing. Every heartbeat:
I wake to awareness of you.

Without

I can't see you, can't touch you
can't breathe, because without you—

but I'm never without you. Even
when all I am is ache.

Especially then. Press my fingers
to the delicate bones of my wrist

and there you are, accompanying me
with every beat of my yearning heart.

Spring

When I remember you
my fingertips tingle.
I'm a lilac, petals
prickling to spring free.

Yearning tangles my tongue.
My words become fragrance.
My heart overflows
like a wadi after a storm.

The thought of you
nourishes me, dizzies me.
Breathe into me
and I bloom.

Rachel Barenblat

Everything I write

Everything I write is a love letter to you.
Some days I'm afraid you don't read them:
that insidious voice whispers in my ear
that even you couldn't possibly want

my graphomanic tendencies. That in writing
day after day I make unreasonable demands.
That my unruly heart takes up too much space.
I can't excise that voice, but I can turn

from the poison it spreads. I remind myself
that you love me not despite who I am
but because of who I am, and that means
all of me. You see my whole heart, even

the parts I try to hide. You don't want me
to pretend. You receive me as I am.

Return again

I wouldn't be here without you.
Because you read, I want to write;
because you listen, I sing again.
How can it already be a year
since the holidays last called me home?
Deep breath, get ready, time to turn.

To everything, turn, turn, turn—
the only thing that's constant is you.
I'm not always sure where to find home.
Sometimes it's in what I write,
the daily chronicle of the old year
manifesting in my poems again.

I know it's time to look again
at where I missed the mark, to turn
my attention toward the old year
for one last time. I know that you
forgive me for the words I didn't write,
times when I couldn't be a home

for you or even for myself. Home
means the safety to start over again,
to shine so that everything I write
illuminates. I want to return
to the safety I find when I'm with you.
I want to live in that place this year.

Rachel Barenblat

What is the thing for which I yearn
the most? Only this: to be at home
in my skin, to be at home with you
in the temple of Shabbat again
and again. To sanctify every turn
my life takes, be brave enough to write

my way to who I really am. Rewrite
my heart, rewire my synapses. This year
I want to see your face at every turn.
Because I'm not alone, I'm always home.
With every heartbeat say thanks again
for enlivening me, for being you.

May the words I write bring me home.
May the new year help me begin again.
May I always turn with love toward you.

Only the beginning

Coming through the sea
was only the beginning.
The giddiness of walking
through walls of living water...

But the story doesn't end there.
Now it's desert, without a map.
What if the next forty years
are bone-dry and desolate?

Maybe it wasn't so bad, that life
numb and familiar. Cucumbers
and fish fresh from the Nile.
Certainty: a fixed path.

Now hope unfolds its mighty wings
and every step risks failure.
When I falter, remind me
I didn't cross the sea alone.

Remind me there's a mountain
I'm heading toward, a promise
that spans lifetimes
of becoming, together, with you.

Rachel Barenblat

Sing me awake

I want to hear your voice
every day of my life.
Murmur in my ear a reminder:
you knock on the door of my heart.

Every day of my life
you bring light to my eyes.
You knock on the door of my heart.
Sing me awake, don't stop.

You bring light to my eyes
and ease my knotted fears.
Sing me awake. Don't stop.
Your melody flows through me.

Ease my knotted fears.
There is no door, only love.
Your melody flows through me.
There is no distance.

There is no door, only love.
Murmur in my ear a reminder
there is no distance.
I want to hear your voice.

Stay

The instant you depart
I'm counting the days.

When I'm wholly with you
everything is sweeter.

A simple swallow of wine
reveals new flavors.

My soul is doubled
like manna in the desert.

My laugh lines deepen.
I am radiant as a bride.

If only I could stop time
and stay in your embrace.

Rachel Barenblat

All I have

All I have is love.
It doesn't feel like enough.
What can I give you?
I'm trying not to hide my light.

It doesn't feel like enough.
(I'm working on this,
and trying not to hide my light.)
What do you need?

I'm working on this:
can't I make offerings?
What do you need
to balm this day?

Can't I make offerings:
rose petals in your path
to balm this day?
I want to lay my words

like rose petals in your path,
the work of my hands.
I want to lay my words
at your feet, to nourish you.

The work of my hands.
What can I give you
at your feet, to nourish you?
All I have is love.

To Shabbes

I want to plead "don't go!"
      though I know you'll return.
            I trust the future I can't see.

My strength is in your song
      even when I'm not certain
            how to play all the chords.

When you're with me
      every channel opens,
            sweetness courses through.

My unlovely thin skin
      becomes a cloak of light.
            I breathe the air of Eden.

Return quickly, beloved!
      I'm counting the days.
            I carry you in my heart.

Rachel Barenblat

Untie my tangles

I come to you tangled.
I come to you hurting
and afraid, my muscles
in knots, my heart sore.

You won't judge me
even if I cry myself ugly.
Even if my circuits are wired
strange. Even if I yearn.

Run your gentle fingers
through me. Loosen
the snarls, the snares.
Remind me how to breathe.

Tell me I'm not too much.
Invite all of me
to walk with you. See me
and I become whole.

Betroth

I want to tell you
        my truths from
                one world to the next.

Help me believe
        you won't grow tired
                of hearing my voice.

I wrap your words
        around my arm,
                imprint you on my skin.

Tuck your words
        into my pocket,
                close to my heart.

If I ignite my words
        will they reach you
                with a sweet savor?

It's all right
        if you don't answer,
                if you can't answer.

Just don't ask me
        to be silent, please
                let me pour out my love.

Rachel Barenblat

This road

I love this road
because it leads to you.

Even when I'm footsore
and weary, the knowledge

that I'm pointed
in your direction

is enough to sweeten
these twists and curves.

When I turn toward you
joy speeds my heart.

Wherever you are
is Eden.

No one like you

I want you to know me
and love me anyway.

I thirst for you
like water after a fast.

There is no one like you.
The joy I find with you —

the rest of my days
wouldn't be enough.

And who I am
when I'm with you —

I want to be that person
every day of my life.

My ribcage splays open:
no holding back.

My beating heart
is yours.

Rachel Barenblat

What lasts

Not the roof. Not
the walls. Not even

my words. The stars
burn out, the hills

erode. But my love
for you was drawn

from the well created
before Eden.

Will never run dry.
Will never wear away.

Open

You are the doorman,
the one I don't notice

holding the heavy panel
so I can go through.

You are the hinge
that swings the door,

the joint and socket
that make opening possible.

You are the door
through which I walk

from one chapter
to the next,

adorned with words
that remind me

who I'm becoming,
who I really am.

Rachel Barenblat

Ascent

Immerse, my body bare as birth.
Emerge with my skin tingling.

Ascend the fifteen stairs to you
singing love songs on every step.

At the door to the holy of holies
I vibrate like a struck bell.

My fears rise up. What makes me think
I'm good enough for you?

Only this: you make me want
to shine as only I can shine.

Let me find favor in your eyes.
I ache to draw near to you.

Nothing I can offer would be enough.
All I have is this heart, bruised

and tender. All I am is this heart,
saying your name with every beat.

That's why

Because I could say your names
tasting them on my tongue
for hours and not grow tired.

Because when you're with me
I sparkle like water in the sun.
Because I turn toward your light.

Because when I remember you
I shine like Moshe come down
from the mountain.

Because my heart, full of you,
bursts open like a ripe fig
juicy and sweet.

Rachel Barenblat

Awaken

You are the shofar
calling me to rise
from my slumber.

You are the voice
of my beloved
knocking at my heart.

You are love
washing over me
like bright moonlight.

You are melody
expanding my heart
until tears come.

You are summer dawn,
the morning I crave
all winter long.

I want you
to wake me up.
Don't ever stop.

About the author

Rachel Barenblat holds an MFA from the Bennington Writing Seminars. She was ordained a rabbi by ALEPH: Alliance for Jewish Renewal in 2011. She received a second ordination from ALEPH as a mashpi'ah ruchanit (spiritual director) in 2012. Selected as a Rabbis Without Borders Fellow in 2013 by Clal (the Center for Jewish Learning & Leadership), she served with Rabbi David Evan Markus as co-chair of ALEPH from 2015-2017, and as interim Jewish chaplain to Williams College in Williamstown, MA, in 2017. She is also a Senior Builder at Bayit: Your Jewish Home.

Barenblat is author of *70 faces: Torah poems* (Phoenicia Publishing, 2011), *Waiting to Unfold* (Phoenicia Publishing, 2013), *Toward Sinai: Omer poems* (Velveteen Rabbi Press, 2016), and *Open My Lips* (Ben Yehuda Press, 2016) as well as several chapbooks, among them *the skies here* (Pecan Grove Press, 1995), *What Stays* (Bennington Writing Seminars Alumni Chapbook Series, 2002), *chaplainbook* (Laupe House Press, 2006), and *See Me: Elul poems* (Velveteen Rabbi Press, 2014.)

Since 2003 she has blogged as The Velveteen Rabbi, and in 2008 her blog was named one of the top 25 blogs on the internet by *Time*. In 2016 the Forward named her one of America's Most Inspiring Rabbis. She is perhaps best known for the (free, downloadable) *Velveteen Rabbi's Haggadah for Pesach*, which has been used in homes and synagogues worldwide.

Her poems have appeared in a wide variety of

magazines and anthologies, among them *Phoebe, The Jewish Women's Literary Annual, The Texas Observer, The Bloomsbury Anthology of Contemporary Jewish American Poetry* (Bloomsbury, 2013) and *The Poet's Quest For God* (Eyewear Publishing, 2014.) You can find her prose in *The Women's Seder Sourcebook* (Jewish Lights, 2002), *God: Jewish Choices for Struggling with the Ultimate* (Torah Aura, 2008) and *Keeping Faith in Rabbis: A Community Conversation on Rabbinical Education* (Avenida, 2014) among other places.

She serves as spiritual leader of Congregation Beth Israel in North Adams, MA. Find her online at velveteenrabbi.com.

More poetry from
Ben Yehuda Press

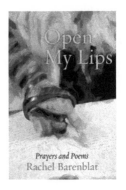

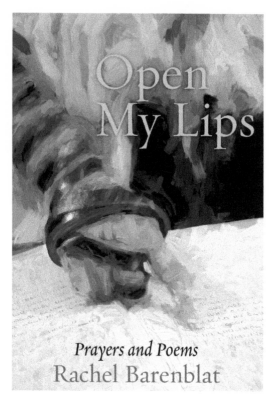

Prayers and Poems
Rachel Barenblat

"'You enfold me in this bathtowel/You enliven me with coffee,' writes Barenblat in this collection of accessible and compelling prayer-poems that manages to locate the sacred in the quotidian. After reading these poems, one realizes the ordinary moment is filled with hidden light, and inspiration isn't as far away as we often assume."
—**Yehoshua November**, author of *God's Optimism*

"Rabbi Barenblat's poems are like those rare cover songs that bring new insights to familiar rhythms and melodies. Her interpretations of ancient liturgy turn up the volume and realign the balance on our tradition's greatest hits."
—**Rabbi Elana Zelony**, Congregation Beth Shalom, San Francisco

Rachel Barenblat

Daily Miracles

You bring my son's footfalls to my door
and shock me awake with his cold heels against my ribs.

You teach me to distinguish waking life from dreaming.
You press the wooden floor against the soles of my feet.

You slip my eyeglasses into my questing hand
and the world comes into focus again.

In the time before time You collected hydrogen and oxygen
into molecules which stream now from my showerhead.

You enfold me in this bathtowel.
You enliven me with coffee.

Every morning you remake me in your image
and free me to push back against my fears.

You are the balance that holds up my spine,
the light in my gritty, grateful eyes.

Seven reasons: Psalm 147

You rebuild your city with our hands
and gather our scattered sparks.
You darn the heels of our hearts
and comfort us with bandages.

You smear sunrise across the heavens
like raspberry jam
and coax every blade of grass
to emerge from the dark comfort of soil.

And you love our fragility
not our particle physics
nor the bridges we labored to plant
across the inlets your glaciers carved.

You lay down ice like glass
and frost like lace on our windowpanes
and then you breathe a January thaw
and our frozen places melt.

Rachel Barenblat

Here and gone

for seudah shlishit, the "third meal" of Shabbat

You're most palpably here
in the moment departure begins.

We turn off the artificial lights,
feel the darkening of the sky.

I'm the deer, caught
in Your presence.

When it grows too dark
we sing without words

and that's what cracks me open.
My cup overflows.

There is nothing but You.
You are everything.

is

heretical Jewish blessings and poems

Yaakov Moshe

FOREWORD BY ANDREW RAMER
AFTERWORD BY JAY MICHAELSON

"What if Rumi or Hafiz were to walk into a poetry workshop? And who (besides God) would be qualified to judge their works? These heretical poems and blessings are succinct and paradoxical, full of laughs and surprises, restoring spiritual wisdom (and foolishness!) to an empty art."

—**Timothy Liu**, author of *Kingdom Come: A Fantasia* and *Burnt Offerings*

Rachel Barenblat

Yedid Nefesh

beloved of my soul
incarnate yourself
not as they say, once in two millennia,
but as i know you
like cain knew his sister
in the transgressive sanctity
of love.

strip yourself of this separation
fill this body
so that there is no distance
between heaven and the earth.

On forgetting God is everywhere

Open my mouth and speak through me.

On heaven and earth there is none else.
But often these words are empty of awe.

One That Is,
grant me the grace of memory,
or shock me anew with the ordinary.

Remind me that this self is nothing more
than a collection of strands of You.
Remind me that it is You looking through these eyes
at Yourself.

If my desires, fears, anxieties are in the way,
help me to see them, and see them as
what is.

Remind me that there is only
the subatomic soup,
or the twenty two letters,
or the four elements —
that whatever map we use,
the territory is either empty

or empty of all but You.

On entering another's place of worship

Light which shines through forms,
Reality of many names,
as we enter this place of holiness,
grant us insight to see you,
grant us balance of mind
to love our own and another's forms
polyamorously for You.

As we uphold ancient precepts
by men scared of idolatry,
guard us from idolatry in our hearts,
which mistake form for Light.

As no form can contain you,
your vastness encompasses multitudes.
As your will is untranslatable,
your essence is beyond concept.
Remain with us, Holy One,
so we may honor our path
and You.

"Intimate and meditative, Shiva Moon has the quality of prayer, yet it's also the journal of a harrowing year, filled with mourning, recollection, and a struggle for spiritual equilibrium. With her celebrated gifts for pictorial and lyrical language (leavened here with Hebrew terms), Maxine Silverman enters the darkness of her beloved father's death and seeks a way to accommodate his loss. This is a wise, moving book for every reader—and a necessary book for anyone who's known loss."

— **Joan Murray**, author, *Swimming for the Ark*

Preview: Yaakov Moshe

What I Learned So Far

When Ellen says my poems these days seem one seamless Kaddish,
I hear she understands the six months
before my father died were raw keen k'riah.

How June's visit home I see his death
forming in the air he breathes.

Why every evening I call him
until there's nothing left to say,
until all that remains—the sheer
pleasure of his company.

Elul. He weakens before my eyes,
no shofar blast required.

        Tishrei. We daven
repetitions to dwell in meaning: who shall live
and who shall die, who in the fullness of years

        We cross into wilderness, a new year,
pillar of fire before us, the old, the weak, the infirm
to the rear, Amalek plucking them one death
at a time.

        Reservations for December.
My father says, "Come right now." and I do.

A way is made.
Gathered to his people,
a story old as time.

Driving Lesson

At twilight and first rainfall
take care.
These moments
bring peril to the road—

  on again brights, off again light,

    creatures dart from the edge of things,

      rain slicks the blacktop grime—

then darkness and the road even out.

What lessons did your father teach?
You heed a man whose brakes snap
in the Rockies, late afternoon sun
aiming fire at the windshield,

who steers the green Chevy between cliff face and gorge,

his girls playing Slap Jack in the back, only tin rail and him
between them and thin-wild air,

coasting to a stop, loosens his grip to flag some help,
orders pan fried steak at Tucker's All Night.

Mostly brakes hold, and luck. All the same, when light falls
or rain, I look for him.

A Mourner's Prayer

How fortunate to buy a white candle,
to know when to strike the match,
shovel dirt and hear it thud
on the lid, to reminisce
over photographs (to have photographs)
and fold his clothes for those less fortunate.

How luxurious to say Kaddish for one person,
letting grief resonate, deep bell tone
thrumming deeper and round.

O Love, reverberate, ricochet.
Loss and longing, lash out.

    She knows precisely who
she weeps for, leaving a stone on his stone
near the stone his father and mother share.

Welcome, Grief,
resident alien, *baruch haba.*
        Memory
will count Father in the minyan
of a daughter's heart.
              Year after year
how privileged to light the candle.
    Most fortunate daughter thanks her father,
tear after tear.